Cambrid
▶ **INTER**

Regina
Series editor: Bob Hastings

BLIZZARDS
KILLER
SNOWSTORMS

A1

Genevieve Kocienda

CAMBRIDGE
UNIVERSITY PRESS

Discovery
EDUCATION

CAMBRIDGE UNIVERSITY PRESS
Cambridge, New York, Melbourne, Madrid, Cape Town,
Singapore, São Paulo, Delhi, Mexico City

Cambridge University Press
32 Avenue of the Americas, New York, NY 10013-2473, USA

www.cambridge.org
Information on this title: www.cambridge.org/9781107621640

First published 2014

Printed in Hong Kong, China, by Golden Cup Printing Company Limited

A catalog record for this publication is available from the British Library.

Library of Congress Cataloging-in-Publication Data

Kocienda, G.
  Blizzards : killer snowstorms : level A1 / Genevieve Kocienda.
      pages cm. -- (Cambridge discovery interactive readers)
    ISBN 978-1-107-62164-0 (pbk. : alk. paper)
  1. Blizzards--Juvenile literature. 2. Readers (Elementary) 3. English language--Textbooks for
foreign speakers. I. Title.

QC926.37.K63 2014
551.55'5--dc23

                        2013013655

ISBN 978-1-107-62164-0

Additional resources for this publication at www.cambridge.org

Layout services, art direction, book design, and photo research: Q2ABillSMITH GROUP
Editorial services: Hyphen S.A.
Audio production: CityVox, New York
Video production: Q2ABillSMITH GROUP

Distributed By:
Grass Roots Press
Toll Free: 1-888-303-3213
Fax: (780) 413-6582
Web Site: www.grassrootsbooks.net

Contents

Before You Read: Get Ready!

Too much snow, wind, and cold can be dangerous.

Words to Know

Complete the sentences with the correct words.

rescue   temperature   freezing   moisture   snowflakes

1 When it snows, you can see _____ in the sky.

2 When water changes to snow, it is _____ cold.

3 _____ is a little water on or in something.

4 The _____ tells us how hot or cold something is.

5 To _____ someone means to make them safe.

Words to Know

Read the paragraph. Then complete the sentences with the correct highlighted words.

Blizzards are dangerous – they damage trees, houses, and people. Too much snow stops cars moving. People can't get out of their cars. Too much snow stops people walking. People sometimes can't get inside, so they stay out in the cold. When it's very cold, people shiver because the body wants to stay warm.

1 A person's _____ is their head, arms, legs, hands, etc.

2 When blizzards _____ trees, sometimes the trees go down and hit the tops of houses.

3 When you _____ , your teeth sometimes make a noise.

4 When something isn't safe, it's _____ .

Video Quest

Blizzards

Watch this video to learn about blizzards. What's the most dangerous thing about a blizzard?

CHAPTER 1

What Is a Blizzard?

WINTER WEATHER CAN BE COLD, WINDY, AND SNOWY. SOMETIMES, THERE IS TOO MUCH SNOW, WIND, AND COLD ALL AT THE SAME TIME.

THIS KIND OF WEATHER IS A BLIZZARD.

A blizzard is a very strong and **dangerous** snowstorm. The snow falls[1] for many hours. The winds are very, very strong – 56 kilometers an hour or more. And the temperature is very low – far below 0° Celsius.[2]

To have a blizzard, there must be three things. First, there has to be cold air. Second, there has to be warm air above the cold air. Third, there has to be lot of moisture in the air.

[1] **fall:** go down; past tense is "fell"
[2] **0° Celsius:** zero degrees Celsius; the temperature when water changes to snow

In a blizzard, heavy snow falls for many hours, or sometimes for many days. In Thompson Pass, Alaska, in 1953, 475 centimeters of snow fell in seven days. On January 25, 2011, in New York City, 48 centimeters of snow fell in two days. The city closed all schools and **airports**.

? ANALYZE

Why did New York City close schools and airports when there was a blizzard?

CHAPTER 2

The Cold

RUSSELL COX KNOWS BLIZZARDS CAN BE VERY DANGEROUS.

In March 2004, Russell Cox and his wife, Brenda, went for a walk in the White Mountains in New Hampshire. The weather in these **mountains** changes quickly. It can be very nice one minute, and very bad a few minutes later.

They walked up near the top of one of the mountains. They were in the clouds. Snow started to fall. At first, the snow was light. When they reached the top, the snow was very heavy.

Russell and Brenda started to walk down the mountain. It was dangerous. They walked into a blizzard. The sky was very gray. Everything was the same color. It was almost impossible to see or walk. Russell and Brenda didn't know where they were!

Because the weather was freezing cold, Russell and Brenda started to get hypothermia.

The body's normal temperature is about 37° Celsius. In very cold weather, the body's temperature can go down below normal. Then, a person cannot think. The heart[3] becomes slow. Breathing[4] becomes slow. This is hypothermia. It is very dangerous. You can die from it.

In hypothermia, the heart becomes slow

[3] **heart:** sends the blood around the body
[4] **breathing:** taking air into the body and out of the body

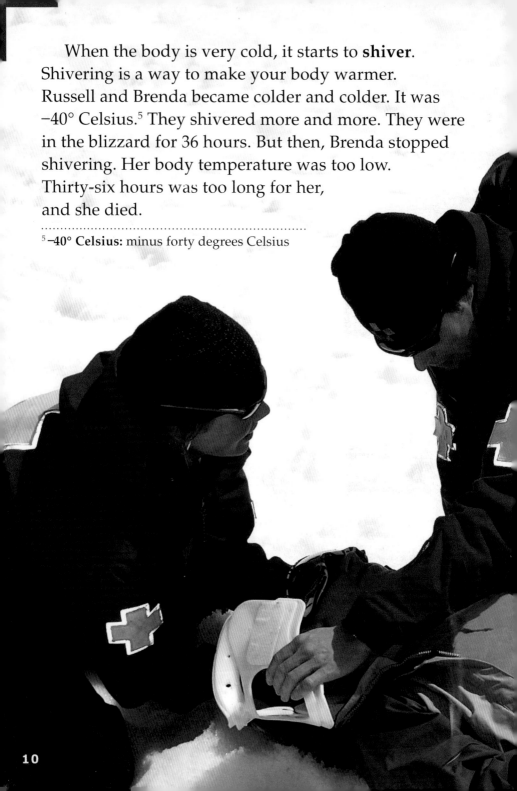

When the body is very cold, it starts to **shiver**.
Shivering is a way to make your body warmer.
Russell and Brenda became colder and colder. It was
−40° Celsius.[5] They shivered more and more. They were
in the blizzard for 36 hours. But then, Brenda stopped
shivering. Her body temperature was too low.
Thirty-six hours was too long for her,
and she died.

[5] **−40° Celsius:** minus forty degrees Celsius

The next morning, people found Russell and **rescued** him. He **survived**, but he was very sick because of the hypothermia. He had frostbite on his feet.

Frostbite comes from very cold temperatures and strong wind. It damages your body. A part of your body, like a hand or foot, freezes and dies. Doctors must take off this part. Russell lost 70 percent of his right foot and 30 percent of his left foot to frostbite.

Russell learned how dangerous cold can be.

Video Quest

Shivering

Watch this video to learn about hypothermia. What are three things that show a person has it?

CHAPTER 3

The Snow

IN A BLIZZARD, THE COLD AIR IS VERY DANGEROUS. PEOPLE CAN GET HYPOTHERMIA AND FROSTBITE. SOMETIMES THEY DIE. SNOW IS ALSO DANGEROUS.

In a blizzard, the snow can fall for many hours or days. It can be very high.

How much snow is too much? In the Pacific Northwest of the United States, about 15 meters of snow falls each year. It has the most snow of all places in the US. The snow is beautiful, clean, and white, but Darryl Jane learned that it is also deadly.[6]

----

[6]**deadly:** very, very dangerous

In November 2006, Darryl Jane was driving his car from Oregon to Washington State. He wanted a quiet day far from the city. The sun was bright and the sky was blue. There was no snow.

Darryl drove higher into the mountains, and snow started to fall. It became very heavy. He was 80 kilometers from any town. He started to feel worried.

Darryl decided[7] to go back home. He tried to turn around, but the car didn't go. The snow was too high. And a terrible[8] blizzard was very close.

....

[7] **decide:** choose
[8] **terrible:** very bad

ANALYZE

Why didn't Darryl leave his car and try to find help?

Darryl left his car to get help, but there was nobody around. Darryl went back to his car. He did the right thing. In a blizzard, a person cannot survive outside for long.

In the morning, over 60 centimeters of snow fell. For over a week, Darryl lived in the car. He had a little food and water with him. He used the car's heater[9] for 15 minutes, two times a day.

....

[9]**heater:** a machine that makes the inside of the car warmer

14

A snowmobile

Darryl waited in his car. On day 9, the snowflakes became very big. This is dangerous because big snowflakes have more moisture. The car was under the snow. Darryl was very worried. He didn't want to die!

On day 15, the blizzard stopped, but Darryl was too tired to leave his car. Then he saw a man on a snowmobile. Someone was there to rescue him!

Darryl lost five kilos, but he didn't have hypothermia or frostbite. He survived.

CHAPTER 4

The Wind

There are often blizzards in the mountains. Why? Because mountains often have two things: snow and wind. Wind in a blizzard is very dangerous. The wind in some strong blizzards goes at more than 72 kilometers an hour.

The wind was 140 kilometers an hour in the Great Lakes storm of 1913! The Great Lakes are large bodies of water between the US and Canada. They have many storms. The storm of 1913 made high waves[10] on the lakes. Twelve ships sank.[11] Over 260 people died in this terrible blizzard.

....

[10]**wave:** water going up and down
[11]**sink:** fall under the water; past tense is "sank"

Snow doesn't always fall in blizzards. Sometimes snow flies into the air. A strong wind can blow[12] snow up into the air. This is a ground blizzard. Patagonia, in South America, is a place that has many ground blizzards.

Near Patagonia, storms start in the ocean.[13] They become very strong and go onto the land. There's a lot of **ice** and snow in Patagonia. Wind from the ocean storms blows the snow and ice up into the air.

....

[12]**blow:** make air go fast
[13]**ocean:** very large body of water

When wind and the cold air come together, the weather can feel colder. This is called the wind chill factor. The wind chill factor isn't the air temperature. It's how cold the temperature feels to a person. For example, on a cold day, the temperature is −6° Celsius. But if the wind is blowing at 40 kilometers an hour, the temperature feels like −26° Celsius. That's a lot colder! People have to wear very warm clothes in cold weather. Hypothermia and frostbite can happen very quickly.

Strong winds make snowdrifts, large piles of snow that the wind forms. Snowdrifts can be many meters high. They're dangerous for cars, buses, and trains. Snowdrifts blow onto roads and train tracks.

When strong winds blow snow around, a whiteout can happen. In a whiteout, it's difficult to see because there's too much snow in the air – everything is white! In the North American blizzard of 2010, New York City had winds of 97 kilometers an hour. No one could see anything but white snow.

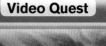

Video Quest

Patagonian Ground Blizzard

Watch this video about some friends who survived a blizzard. What three things did Steve and Chad do to survive?

CHAPTER 5

What Do You Think?

DO YOU LIVE IN A PLACE WITH BLIZZARDS? DO YOU KNOW WHAT TO DO IN A BLIZZARD?

Think about this: You live in an apartment in a city. You're watching TV. On the **news**, they say a terrible blizzard is coming. It's going to snow for three days. The snow is going to start in about two hours. The wind is going to be 65 kilometers an hour.

Your sister is still at school, and your parents are at work. You have a little food in the kitchen, but not a lot. What do you do first? What do you do next?

First, call your family and tell them to come home. In a blizzard, it's very important to be inside. Then, go to a store and buy water, a flashlight, and batteries. Buy food that will stay good for a long time – food in cans.

Stay warm. Get a lot of clothes and blankets. Try to find a radio with batteries, too. You want to hear important news.

Remember – blizzards are dangerous. But if you do the right things, you can survive.

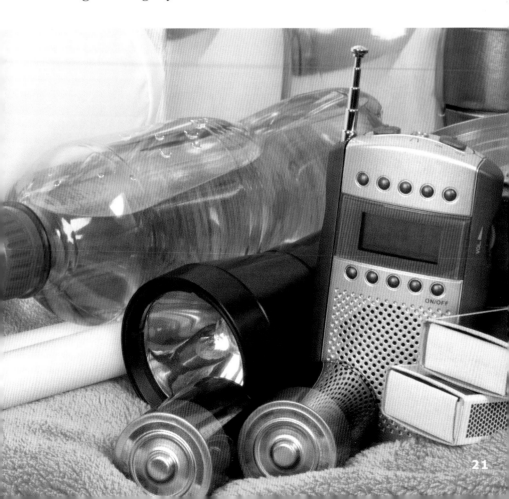

After You Read

Read the sentences and choose Ⓐ (True) or Ⓑ (False).

1 In a blizzard, winds are under 56 kilometers an hour.
- Ⓐ True
- Ⓑ False

2 A blizzard needs warm air and cold air.
- Ⓐ True
- Ⓑ False

3 If it snows heavily for only one hour, it is not a blizzard.
- Ⓐ True
- Ⓑ False

4 There has to be a lot of moisture in the air for a blizzard to form.
- Ⓐ True
- Ⓑ False

5 The body's normal temperature is below 37° Celsius.
- Ⓐ True
- Ⓑ False

6 In hypothermia, blood moves faster.
- Ⓐ True
- Ⓑ False

Video
7 If you stay outside in a blizzard, it is dangerous to stop shivering.
- Ⓐ True
- Ⓑ False

8 In a blizzard, a person cannot survive outside for a long time.
- Ⓐ True
- Ⓑ False

Match

Match the vocabulary with the correct definitions.

Words	Definitions
1 dangerous _____	a. make someone safe
2 temperature _____	b. very, very cold
3 rescue _____	c. your body does this when it's cold
4 shiver _____	d. how hot or cold something is
5 freezing _____	e. not safe
6 moisture _____	f. water on or in something

Answer the Questions

Read pages 6–19 again and answer the questions.

1 Where was Russell when the blizzard came?

_____

2 Who rescued Darryl?

_____

3 What part of the body does frostbite damage?

_____

4 Why does the body shiver in cold weather?

_____

5 What happens in a whiteout?

_____

Answer Key

Words to Know, page 4
① snowflakes ② freezing ③ Moisture ④ temperature
⑤ rescue

Words to Know, page 5
① body ② damage ③ shiver ④ dangerous

Video Quest, page 5
cold air

Analyze, page 7
Because 48 centimeters of snow fell in two days.

Video Quest, page 11
Answers will vary.

Analyze, page 14
Because there was nobody around, and in a blizzard a person cannot survive outside for long.

Video Quest, page 19
They put up a tent to get away from the cold and wind. They lived in their tent for two weeks. They tried to move the snow from their tent every day.

True or False, page 22
① B ② A ③ A ④ A ⑤ B ⑥ B ⑦ A ⑧ A

Match, page 23
① e ② d ③ a ④ c ⑤ b ⑥ f

Answer the Questions, page 23
① in the mountains of New Hampshire
② a man on a snowmobile
③ a hand or foot
④ to make itself warmer
⑤ Snow blows hard, and you can't see anything.